Everything 1 The Sur

by Marcia S. Freeman

rourke
Educational Media
rourkeeducationalmedia.com

Have you ever played a guessing game? In one game, if you are IT, you think of something and everyone else must try to guess what it is.

Is it a chair?

Is it a cheetah?

For sure, the thing you think of will be **matter**. Matter is everything under the sun. It's all the stuff we find on earth and in space.

Matter takes up space and has weight. It can be as light as feathers or as heavy as metal.

You are made of matter. You take up space and you have weight.

We can **sort** all the matter in the world into groups. For example, we can say that matter is a **liquid**, a **solid**, or a **gas**.

You are part liquid, part solid, and part gas. Blood, bones, and the air you breathe or a burp!

Bubbles are transparent.

We can sort matter into stuff that lets light through or stuff that blocks light. If light can go through it, we say the matter is **transparent** or **translucent**.

Goggles and glasses are transparent. Some shower doors and this frosted car windshield are translucent.

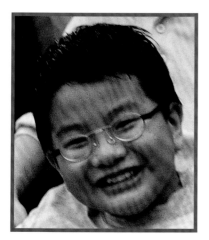  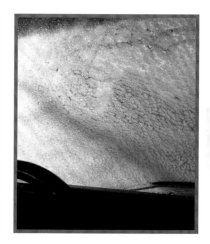

What is the difference between transparent and translucent?

If light cannot go through matter, we say it is **opaque**. (Opaque rhymes with cake)

We can sort matter into living and non-living stuff. Plants and animals are living matter.

Non-living matter is stuff that was alive once or never was alive. Wood comes from trees that once grew.

But, pennies or plastic pails were never alive.

11

Some matter is **edible** and some is not.

Please do not eat the fork. It is not edible.

Some matter is soft and warm. We can use it to make clothes.

Some matter is strong and **sturdy**. We can use it for shoes and boots.

Some matter is so strong we can use it to build things.

Matter is everything under the sun. It is everything we need.

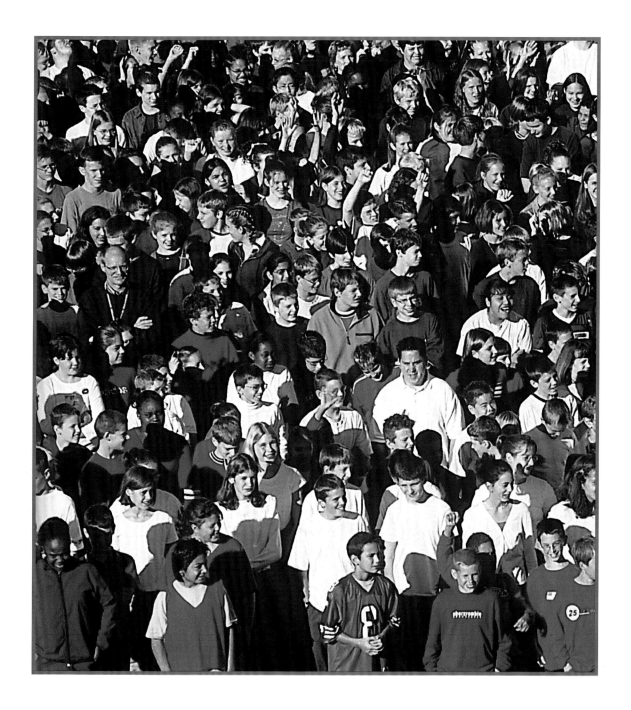

Glossary

edible	something that can be eaten
gas	a form of matter, often invisible, that can expand
liquid	matter that you can pour
matter	something that has weight
opaque	matter that blocks light
solid	matter you can not pour
sort	group things
transparent	matter that you can see through
translucent	matter that lets light through but you can't see through it

Definitions

Index